SOME BODIES

IN THE

GRIEF BED

POEMS BY

RICK BENJAMIN

SOME BODIES

IN THE

GRIEF BED

POEMS BY

RICK BENJAMIN

Homebound Publications
Ensuring that the mainstream isn't the only stream.

HOMEBOUND PUBLICATIONS

WWW.HOMEBOUNDPUBLICATIONS.COM

HOMEBOUND PUBLICATIONS IS A REGISTERED TRADEMARK OF HOMEBOUND PUBLICATIONS

© 2021 TEXT BY RICK BENJAMIN

Published in 2021 by Homebound Publications
Cover Design and Interior Design by Leslie M. Browning
ISBN: 978-1953340047
First Edition Trade Paperback

10 9 8 7 6 5 4 3 2 1

Look for our titles in paperback, ebook, and audiobook wherever books are sold. Wholesale offerings for retailers available through Ingram. Homebound Publications and its divisions are distributed by Publisher's Group West.

Homebound Publications, is committed to ecological stewardship. We greatly value the natural environment and invest in environmental conservation. For each book purchased in our online store we plant one tree.

for Sharon Barovsky, Bruce Burnett, & Bonnie Markham
—with gratitude

for my students, past & present
—my good fortune to think & learn among you

All grief is beauty; grief is about making life

— MARTÍN PRECHTEL

I'm alive, right—don't we say that?
We don't think about the bones we walk on.

—KŪKAI

CONTENTS

KINTSUGI

for Deanna Nikaido

A shattered elbow,
shoe-horn cracks
in psyches from
some childhood
brutalities, too
many broken
windows
to count.

There is an art
to putting pieces
back in their
places. *A* golden
web keeps every
vessel intact. For
every injury,
a healing.

HARDWARE, FLOWERS

for Luke Daniel Benjamin

The grandson of the man
who first opened Durfee's

Hardware doesn't know
the name of all the tools

& your Pop, who doesn't
suffer fools in hardware

stores gracefully, asks
to talk to the old man.

He needs someone who
can tell when hundred-

year old windows need
chain not rope, weights

dropping down as panes of
wavy glass slide up.

:: :: ::

Gary Snyder says, *learn the
flowers, go light,* & I know

he's right, but what if the
flowers he knows are

vanishing at a rate faster
than we can remember

their names, faster
than a fight to keep

fate from dropping
roots to what always

disappears? Because
it isn't just chains,

or trains of thought,
or some bloom's scent

we still smell even
without knowing it.

It's all the things we
can't repair, don't

know the names of
any more. It's every

door, & the missing
hardware & the fact

that you & everyone
you love is still going

to have to walk
through it.

NO DEPOSIT ZONE

Also known as "NDZ,"
within the NDZ may not

discharge any sewage,
treated or untreated, into
Narragansett Bay, as in

ships, which *here*, on
this map, are the vessels
being referred to, as in,

I'm thinking, *human*
bodies, too, & all
of our own deposits,

treated or untreated:
dioxins, metals,
bacteria, as in

Refugio, refuge, the name
Verrazano gave to this place
when he first laid eyes on it.

As in walking out the front
door of my house, on *Bayside*
Avenue, west side, where

the Pawtuxet flows into the
Providence & together they
join the Bay, 147 miles on

the North Side of Rhode Island
Sound. &, though here, so near
the city, is brackish at best, not

fit to swim in, I wake each
morning to the smell of water,
to sugar caked in a bowl from

exposure to sea-air, to sounds
of ocean birds singing hymns
to their elements. When we

moved two miles out for air &
water for me it meant
returning to the Pacific, to my

first Bay, San Francisco, to
that time I once took visually
impaired kids out to sea for salmon

& the weather-man who would
later feature us on his weather
report—one salmon each

for the sightless—
berated me for not
reminding the kids

to throw up off the *side*
of his father's boat not
in it, for not reminding

them to *look at the horizon
line!*, & I had to remind *him*
that they couldn't *see* it,

though I also remember what
the Bay looked like that day,
boat small as a buoy cresting

over tall waves. Even a year
after the flood when I walked
along the river behind Rhodes

on the Pawtuxet toward Shaw's
Market which would remain
closed for 18 months because

the river ran down all of its aisles,
I still saw remnants of raw sewage
high up in trees, toilet paper

& what was human still clinging
to it: smell of waste still wafting
up from the water & down

from branches that would
not be free of discharge
for a very long time. If you

follow the West Passage
just past the horn at Sand Point
you come to islands named, *Patience,*

Prudence, though others have kept
their native tongues: *Aquidneck,*
Conanicut, words with undeniable

currents to the past running
through them. Where seven
rivers run into the Bay

we call, *sub-drainage basins.*
It is in the nature of this Bay
to remember its tributaries,

holding its three ancient
river valleys in its body,
glacial: ice & rising salt-

water making, *sea-level.*
This morning on this
West end of the Bay, no

vessels seem to be
discharging unless
it is the swans or

my dog swimming
out to meet them. An
egret stands on one foot,

in meditation. I make
in my mind a bridge
to the East Passage.

Some day soon I will
paddle, let current
carry me out beyond

the Sound to a state
that will remain nameless,
where fresh water circulates

in salt water a *tidal*
mixing, a meeting
to make this estuary,

refugio, where it's still possible,
some moments,
light bouncing off water,

gulls slanting in air or
calling out their ancient hungers, to feel one's

body as a vessel keeping
what it has to *itself* for
once, buoyant as anything

else on this Bay without
even a single line
of horizon to see.

BY-PRODUCT STORAGE TANKS

After Joseph Stella

In the museum I (do we say,)—
snap?— a picture of Stella's

industrial sketch in charcoal
(the right material to make

these marks) just before
security says, *no pictures,*

please, sir, even with your
phone. Only later do I see

my own bare scalp reflected
in framed glass before tanks,

back-lit—gray-scale sky ill-
uminating city-scape—

accident, kindred attempt
to contain the human,

the back of my body
surfacing from the tank's

face. Another time I've stored
myself in some unexpected

place, in Stella's sketch,
breaking the rules,

photographing myself
trespassing into work

I've been drawn to.

WHILE WALKING IN THE BUTTERFLY PAVILION

for Luke Daniel Benjamin

Mexican blue wing butterflies like
shade over light, have bodies that
are dark not bright, hover over
bark not blooms, find ways

of scaling any wall, no matter
how tall, just like migrants we
call, *illegal* will. When a
government builds 600 miles

of fencing in the lower Rio Grande
River Valley, substituting
a hard border for the forest
butterflies are used to they

lose a kind of law & order,
nesting & flight patterns
disturbed. For some it means a
slight detour in the middle

of a 2,000 mile pilgrimage,
for many others it means
nothing less than the loss
of a village, homing instincts

rendered useless as a broken
GPS. No one really means to
pillage, of course, simply
hoping to keep those other

immigrants from going north.
Their names come from
humans: *Checkered White,
Northern Cloudywing, Texas*

*Powdered Skipper, Dark Kite
Swallowtail, Mimosa Yellow,* &
*border bandits, field rats, tire
huggers, wetbacks:* One

way or another these parts
of ourselves we give names
to always get in, migrate north
of any place we've ever been

reclaim those forgotten
names we left behind:
butterfly,
mariposa.

I PREFER TO KNOCK ON WOOD

but veneer will always do; you just
must say, *veneer,* so the world knows
you're not pretending authenticity.

Everywhere I look in this coastal
desert something grows here
against its own grain: eucalyptus,

some of the pines, even
fennel. By this point I have
knocked on more trunks

of trees that don't belong here
more times than I can count.
Still, when monarchs

find a resting-place
among groves seeded
by someone's mistake

that breaks into one's
idea of what *home* means,
even if also just another

space created by water
California barons robbed
from nearby river valleys

or, later, rivers from far-
off states. Even if monarchs
don't migrate any place near

LA, humans do, imagining
some easier sort of life though
not even allowing themselves

to hope for it, having already
seen how all the movies that
come from that city end:

knock on *longing*, knock on
some new sense of *belonging*,
knock on all the hard things

not one of us leaves behind.
Knock on anything near-kin
To wood you can find, all

the palm-fronds your own
palms have held, plied wood
or even those other composites

glue holds without a speck
of even saw-dust keeping
them together. Knock on

it holding onto all of your
purest dreams, the ones
you are too afraid to talk

about, the ones you hedge
with your knuckles pressed
to somewhere else you wish

to visit, no time
soon, but *some*
time, only if

you're lucky.

BLESSING THE MIGRATIONS

May the gray whale & her calves
find their way north of Mexican
breeding grounds all the way
to the Bering Sea, in Alaska,
where their ritual feeding
belongs to summer. May their
songs reach other pods more
than a thousand miles away
with news about how safe
are passages, how their stays in
colder water seem fruitful this
year or not, even if what they
haven't got is silence, made to
listen through static humans
have created most days, crossed
wires, if what they haven't got is
navigation undisturbed by a
desire to end their lives. &,
speaking of lives of humans,
may mothers, fathers, & babies
grounded at borders protected
by fear of others find their way
back together, endure these
long separations in colder,
northern waters so far from

home. May they roam like
creatures across a fettered but
freer earth among others who
wish them well, who do not
believe in borders, who are
determined to listen through
static as they ensure a safer
passage to places worth this
brave walking, where, from
coastlines, you can still see gray
whales making their own
unlikely migrations north, also
against the odds, finding their
way, discovering kindred pods
singing the same songs. May we
discover, on land or from sea to
shining sea, that we belong
together, in life after life never
parted.

LESSON

The teacher said, *put your hand over
your heart*, said, *ready, begin*, & we
did begin, saying some thing we'd
memorized without

thinking about it. Only later did
it occur to me that we were not
one nation under god, that there
wasn't liberty & justice

for all, that sometimes it's best not
to pledge allegiance when bad
things are happening in your
country. I mouthed or

didn't even form some words each
morning, knowing them not to be
true. I'd like to think all the gods
smiled down on me.

I'd like to think
that dissent's
also why we still
stood up.

THE WORLD I LIVE IN

Has swallows' nests in it so numerous
neighbors complain about bird shit on
cars & driveways, & unsuspecting

students dodge darting birds
who dive from trees protecting young as
if there will be no tomorrow

without such vigilance. Speaking of
tomorrow, the world I live in is
dangerous, perhaps even more

dangerous than before. A man
wants to build a wall to keep some
others out, insults another

man who, like him, hoards
bombs. Me, I like my cup
of dark-roast in the morning

with a little cream, look up, as I
leave the house, at the industrious
swallows & their hundreds of nests

clinging to the eaves of our houses.
It's all too messy for the people who
live next door. They want cars

they don't have to wash every day,
but drought, I think, means you
don't have to, get to leave it all

alone, & send up prayers, now
& then, that those dangerous
men will also just let lives be.

OTHER DIRECTIONS TO MY HOUSE

for Juan Felipe Herrera

Step back into groves
of avocado trees
so plentiful hundreds
of years ago some
 fruit fell to ground

to feed the earth.
Walk south on dirt
paths fast becoming
sidewalks, roads,
houses. In front
of one of them

is a tree I do not
know the name of I
fell from once. It
almost took my breath
away. Spend a moment

or two there looking
for blood, that trail
your family took
through a city named
after angels to some-

where we hovered like
humming-birds over
some sweetness until
darting away because
there was none to be
had.

TORSO IN OCEAN

Suppose the sea
pulled you down

when you were seven
instead of salting you

up into resuscitating
air? Say you stared

into eyes of your own
drowning self, now

floating somewhere into
some indefinite future?

Suppose the cure for death
was simply dying

toward a new life,
every person you'd

ever lost waiting
to greet you without

needing to breathe in
anything from the past?

Say you were free, free
at last of every

element that ever held
you up or down,

crown of your head
suddenly bursting out

of a new canal, as if
born again, only,

this time, in
to nothing?

THE BODY

has the mind
of an elephant:
it won't forget.

Some nights
a long ago bruise,
some a caress, &,

some days, remembering a
long summer, say as a
teenager, its fierce hunger

wants feeding. Then again,
you're older now. Fact is, gravity
is bringing you down

so some days all you want is
for the air you breathe in to
make you more buoyant,

more likely to skim the surface
of your life-pollen settling on
a rim of water, no threat

of sinking. Of course, you're
thinking, no one wants to grow
 old dying. Better to age

while feeling most alive, body
still remembering that ivory
touch, lifting its old trunk.

ROCK-WALLS TO THE TRAIN-TRACKS

After bike-ride to what we called, *base-camp*
beginning to climb, finding footholds, fossils,
layers of history or prehistory softly coming

apart in our hands. Moving through stands of
low-slung Manzanita, scratching our faces &
arms through the fierce-rooted chaparral.

We summited to train tunnel, tracks, stripping wet
shirts off our backs, placing them on the rails to dry
&, later, to be sliced by locomotives. It was

some other boy lost half his body there I heard,
trading flesh for fabric, not heeding warnings our
parents must have issued. If, in fact, they

ever knew where we'd gone, those days finding
danger in all of the right places. Throwing rocks
against passing trains, them bouncing sharply

back against our own, free & neglected bodies.

FIG TREE IN A FALLEN CITY

Indigenous to Syria, it made
its way most recently to my
hometown, Los Angeles, as if
it belonged in arid places all
over the world, even its most
western edges, where survival
seemed less likely. When I fell
from one once, my left knee
met one metal stake on its
way down that also didn't
belong there. I had no
business being in it in the
first place, thousands of years
removed from what was
indigenous & having no
appreciation then for a fruit
that tasted like sweetness of
ancient loam, or a tree that
could find itself a new home
most anywhere. Now I care a
lot how anything came to be
here or there, how far so
many of us have traveled to
become who we are, mostly
transplants, discovering our

selves rooted to the most un-
likely places & bearing fruit
proud of its plainness, lines
of age older than this time.

ELWOOD

Homes to owls, coastal pines
still their nervy needles even
in wind, bend don't break,
send scent thick as smoke
through the window come
evening. There was a time
darkness & wind & sight
of yellow eyes would've kept
me awake at night. As it was
I wept most times waiting
for that hurricane to blow
through my defenses: cover
pulled tight around my body,
back to wall, knowing an end
was near.

The thing itself is easy: spirit
leaves body, disappears to its
hiding-place where it can still
witness what happens. Mean
time, a boy will wait long as it
takes to find a sleep in which
he's left alone, dreams beyond
something he cannot believe is

actually happening. So many
years asking, who? after night
creatures in the pines.

ELWOOD STORM

An inch of rain
per hour makes
flash floods, &
mud slides hills
down soft as an
avalanche of soil.

It can't, it won't
hurt to lay face
flat to the earth
just this once, &
come up with a
mask you're born

to wear: humility
& dirt, clay red
as rain you once
were & fell from
so full of it, so in
water, mud, love.

SOUNDS OF ELWOOD

Waves fall through
sleep below bluffs
beyond pine,
eucalyptus, sage
brushing against
dreams just loud
enough some
mornings I wake
rested rather than
haunted.

When I don't hear
them sleep might
never come at all.
Instead I might fall
into memories so bad
any sound sounds
like footsteps loud
enough to keep boys
awake, or, worse,
wanted.

Silence is more than
some people can

take, arouses fear,
makes them more
likely to listen for
any murmur,
whispers from
mouths that can't
leave flesh
unwanted.

Me: men on hogs
hot summer nights,
fire between their
legs, put me to sleep
as if din of unmuffled
motors lulled like
ocean all along, &,
I, a boy, stayed
unmolested,
undaunted.

ELWOOD ON A WARM DAY IN APRIL

Wind blows bulrush almost
flat. Beneath the bluffs one
spout, then two—gray whales
making their spring migration
north.

Ahead, a dog finds a path
of scent & follows it far as
it threads to shallow-
rooted eucalyptus. High
above us

a hawk catches updrafts,
rides circles in air. A last
freight train makes its
way through Old-town
after dark.

Another owl sounds
night in a coastal pine.
The smell of sage &
skunk lead us back
some other place

we do not know.

FREEDOM

Our small boy bodies crawling
through dirt between floor
& foundation, finding tortoises hibernating
in corners all winter long,

their sudden intake of breath
a hiss of song that felt like
whispered reminders we
could survive any season,
even this one. Was our father

wrong to bring them back
from Mojave, these
creatures hiding out
in shells withstanding
the hottest surfaces on earth?

It was for certain against
the law to take them
from where they
belonged. But hearing
them sleep in that crawl-space

beneath our house, rage all around us, that moment
I knew only safety,

silence, a place where one
might hear even the softest

breathing out.

THE BIOGRAPHER SPEAKS

What you have been keeping secret
from me you have also been keeping
secret from your self, &, speaking

of yourself, when was the last time
you accounted for what you've done
or left undone, looked at the used-

up heart, took inventory of valves,
arteries, health of the muscle's pulse
long enough to listen to deep bass-

lines thrumming up-spine & through
the blood in your veins? I'm tired
of telling the same stories fired

from the same fictions, as if you
haven't lived through them, dark
as hidden caverns, lit only by sparks

of words you come up with now &
then, of telling truths you only bear
mostly in dreams: the way hair

burns & smells as it turns to smoke,
what it feels like to leave the body
while still watching it from a lobby

safely removed from cheap motels
someone's made of it. You speak
in riddles, rhymes, keep oblique

the hardest lessons as if you can
turn them into words that sing
far into a future that doesn't ring

around your life the way a child's
memories do. Take heart. It all
comes out in the end. The fall

from grace, release from denial
& forgetfulness arrives in its own
good time. Remembered. Known.

LET THEM SAY

After Lucille Clifton

he blushed before
mirrors, lights, both

of which he avoided,
that some nights

memories of what
happened to his body

at the hands of others
would keep him awake,

that if he measured
his temperature any

time of day it would
be a degree or two

above normal, that
someone once said

he didn't look good
in formal clothes, so

he learned never to
dress in them, that

he closed his eyes in
showers every other

day when he shaved
his skull, felt again a

drum on his head &
also the hum in his

heart that was blood
rushing through it,

&, that after all was
said & done it was

much more
than enough.

SELF EXAMINATION IN THIRD PERSON

after Yannis Ritsos

Walking down stairs his left knee whimpers
most mornings, especially cold ones, joints
forecasting weather better than newscasters

or almanacs. He moves toward a counter
& wonders why it's called that, as if surfaces
where we prepare food are all we will ever

know about time. Then a grind of coffee, no
precise measurements just an intuitive sense
of how much water to roasted beans

which before that were berries growing
in volcanic soil on islands in Indonesia.
An eruption can ruin a whole year's crop,

not to mention loss of lives, houses, so much
disappearing in the scalding air. He thinks
of conversations coffee growers must have

daily with volcanoes above them, asking both
for fertility & restraint, for rich dark soil, for
fiery earth staying contained in a hollowed-

out cone. He fingers a single stone in his
pocket to remind himself how close earth
always is to our wanting hands,

stands up to pour from the hot darkness
his body craves first thing each morning,
his mug another kind of cone, & warmth

beginning to seep through his body like lava
cutting another path or road that
only older, calloused feet can hope to walk.

IMAGINARY AUTOBIOGRAPHY

I tread lightly on tips
of branches called *canopy*.
Old sequoias held my weight
as if I was an insect, or a
feathered creature, or a
drop of rain.

More than twice I fell,
slipped off branches, felt
some unyielding ground
rise up to meet me. I can
stay earthbound, crane
a neck for only so long,

must climb to even
thin limbs if I have
a mind to. Up high
there's humming
at my feet, honey
in head & heart

of any
old tree

I ever
climbed
or longed
to live in.

HIS NAME

Home with fever I found ink-pad,
stamp with his name on it, then
pressed it all over a walnut dresser

I now know was veneer. It took
most of half a day to cover every
surface, to mark drawers & a top

I could barely reach with a
name that did not ever belong
to me. Later, he came home &

in a rage to know who had inked
his first & last name onto fake
wood. Maybe fever answered,

body still so hot I spoke
in tongues; maybe since
it was *his* name appeared

everywhere I considered
myself innocent of a crime;
perhaps thinking of crimes

he'd already or would go on
to commit, I'd already up &
pardoned myself, *innocent,*

simply stamped it out right
while I was doing it. In any
case, I lied, I was exonerated.

A FEW STATEMENTS ABOUT THE SOUL

Stagnant or not, water has it, roiling
down-rock or so still in a pond pollen
gathers on its face like dust swept from
trees. &, speaking of trees, I believe in
their sentient exhaling of what we,
ourselves, need in order to breathe
on this earth. It is late, & late at night
I hear the song of stones rolling up &
down beach, soul-clapping castanets,
sound I can live with as long as there
are waves to bring them in. Stones &
trees & water & whatever inside of me
has a kindred tongue to sing with them.
All of us old, all of us old, dear souls.

AN EYEBROW
after Jane Hirshfield

 An eyebrow is not a soft hill
of hair below the forehead,
not foreshadowing of eye's
glimmer, not a frown just
in front of a louder form
of dissatisfaction. Nor is it
a painter's single line above
both eyes & the bridge of
nose, her mark of beauty
& fame, of love from a man
who could not even keep
to that singular line. An
eyebrow is not a deep
questioner though it may
rise up curiously like one
as if asking after a secret
or maybe bits of gossip.
It lifts up sometimes so I-
ronically it's loud as mouth
letting loose a sharp tongue,
but no one really gets hurt.
It keeps codes of silence—
even in dirt.

DRINKING DARK-ROAST IN MY LATE FIFTIES

Breath whistles as it
touches a surface

cooling to its touch.
Second or seconds

later a first sip, beginning
at lip of a new day &

ending back of throat
so full there is a song

in swallowing. Taste
of volcanic soil, taste

of ripe berries, taste
of some thickening

from sleep becoming
thinner & simmering

back to life. Headlines,
stories in *The Times*,

assimilating war
in Syria, crimes

worth noting or
not, eight men

put to death so
fast in Arkansas

in order to beat an
expiration date on

a sedative they
use in executions.

I hold each sip
in my mouth

as if it matters, as
if cultural collapses

can be staved off
with a harvest of

green berries, fire,
the perfect grind.

But, still I mind
everything outside

of the mug, each
act of violence

I am reading about,
the sound of trash

& recycling being
collected outside

dawn-sounds
of insomniac owls

in Coastal pines,
& this no-longer-

sweet elixir bringing
me in to another

day both shorter &
longer than I need it to be.

TO MY DOPPELGANGER

You sit on the curb without knowing what
you are going to do while I start climbing
a tree toward a nest I will never actually
find. You, you're of a mind to follow

directions, rules, to be dutiful before
authority. I disobey, routinely fail to
read instructions, walk away when
someone else tells me what to do.

We're both walking the same road,
that's true, without having any idea
of where we are headed. You ask
each person you meet for directions,

anxious for answers, while I enjoy
getting lost, forget where I meant
to travel, land in someone's kitchen
drinking tea. You have grown tired

of me, always leading you to another
path you'd rather not have followed,
playing it close to the vest, me, still
out to prove we came from one nest.

BROTHERS

For half a century
Yoruba, in Nigeria,

killed one twin
at birth, cursed

with two of some-
thing they wanted

only one of & mothers
of the lost ones made

of their grief dolls they
called, *Ibiji.*

My brother & I
always wondered

which was which,
meaning wanted

or not. We each
called the other,

loved one.

YOU CAN HAVE

after Barbara Rass

You can have forsythia
making you forget you
don't really like the color,
yellow, a 23-year-old son's
hand on your bare head
anointing it like sunlight,
one ripe orange in your
palm when you think
you've reached the point
you can't take any more
days of snow, &, then,
another day of snow.

You can have soft lips
on your cheek when
you're not quite ready
to wake up, whisper
saying you are loved,
the pain in your side
that may mean some-
thing or not, to know
there is also no ending
or beginning to it.

You can have your twin
still facing you as if with-
out him you have no self,
& you can learn to live
without a strong sense
of one even if you still
see him in the mirror.

& You can have bayous
so green your own eyes
soften to the same color,
trees budding in spring,
pine forest, even forsythia
just before it does its thing.

THE FACE TO THE VOICE

for Yusef Komunyakaa

I won't grimace on account
of the pain you're sounding,
but may *give* you the choice
of down-turned lip-edges or
tightening jaws rounding a
sharpening you can't quite
suppress. Sure, I know your
job's to find a song for *every*
mood: that lift when one son
shows up without warning
for a birthday, or the long
sigh of missing that some
one else who isn't there, a
breath that brings you back
to your childhood heavy as
wisteria on a wet night, the
warm undertone whenever
she's about. Why is it your
job, though, to spout off any
little thing you're feeling, ex-
pecting me to find the right
expression for whatever you
might be dealing with— a
spark of anger, the sadness

closing your throat, a tune
whose longing brings that
wistful look of nostalgia to
the eyes? Look, it isn't as if
I'm sending out spies to find
your every tone. Sometimes,
same as you, I just want not
to be looked at, &, for once,
to be left alone.

FOR MY SON

for Gil Langston Benjamin

That time I lost
my patience be

cause you were
acting like me &

I wished I could
spare you all that

except for the part
that was all about

you.

ODE TO MY DAUGHTER'S FEET

for Sarah Jewell Benjamin

Second toe, like mine, longer than what
we call the *big* one, which both of us say,
is *more evolved*. Like me, she is always

hurting them, finding bruises sore on soles,
bone spurs on ankles, more or less constantly
stubbing toes. Who knows *why*. Maybe some

of us simply try to walk with more conviction
in this world & suffer for it, or maybe we're
just stumbling or muddling through it, finding

every slippery rock, exposed root, the crumbling
curb. When she was a child she'd start to climb
mountains & end up being carried up them,

tiring easily. Now she skips up or down more
or less breezily, as if resigned to the next fall.
If that was all there was to it I'd laugh myself,

but my own feet have long since begun to feel
the weight they carry, to slip into shoes, or,
heaven help us, boots, with a greater sense

of the fate that awaits them down-path.
Only sometimes there's an unexpected brook
or river down below, & we throw ourselves

into it as if our feet might become young again,
healed from the pain of living in this uncertain
terrain. Some days that cooling off is all we need

in the way of a reprieve from these hot trails, from
the way the body sometimes fails to find its balance
or breaks like any other impossibly fragile thing.

So we do, don't we, we play out the string as if
every step matters, as if finding foot-bones
in tatters is what was always supposed to happen,

our longer, second toes, having known it
all along.

ODE TO MY GRANDFATHER'S HANDS

Fingered & twisted parts in slant-sixes,
put tools to hundreds of V-6's & V-8's,

came late to air-cooled &
rotary engines. They were large,

his hands, some said, *huge; when*
one of yours was in one of his he

squeezed it like he meant it, &
said, it seems good to see you.

All those years of moving
from one apartment into

a cheaper one somewhere else
in the city & every gang-

banger had his back, slumped
over their engines even after

a long day of work. He loved
engines the way some people

love bodies & it broke him
when car factories started

turning out cars built
to fall apart, fueling

a craving for the new.
Yes, it was true, his

own vehicles hit half-
million miles routinely,

testified to something
made to last & also to

the skills of the man
repairing it. Holding

his soft, calloused hand
in mine was just about

all the fixing I ever
needed those days.

DUTCH RUB

His knuckles dug
deep into my scalp
friction & heat, pain
I'd learn to grow
into. Who knew
what the Dutch had
to do with it? How
some of the men in
my family showed
affection until a kid
cried out & a mother
or grandmother said
that kind of playing
was too rough. Now,
every other day I
shave my head in a
shower with my eyes
closed, feeling that
friction as the hair,
once again, a razor
rubs off, this self-
imposed ritual not
unlike a kind of love.

LATE POEM TO MY GRANDMOTHER

The way you mixed up metaphors
& maxims was epic: pennies, saved
for hundreds of days, *saved nine,*
the shoe fit someone who'd never
worn shoes before & whose
callouses were a testament
to solid ground, & someone who
had a heart of bronze also got his
just desserts. When Roger Maris's
hair fell out in 1961 from stress
of hitting more home runs than
an icon, you said he made *life*
worth loving, & you did, love, your
life more when he set a new bar
for scaling walls, even if only on
a playing field. &, see, here I am
again at the assisted living center.
It's a Monday, Grandma. I am in
the company of my wise elders:
trying to catch a falling star once
more before my heart flames out.

WHAT IS IT LIKE?

What is it like to lay awake,
sleepless, night after night,
wind finding in rain-gutters

groans gathered deep in
metal throats, owls making
their sounds until daybreak

in coastal pines? What is it like
to wake up tired after witnessing
wakefulness while others were

sleeping in the dark, to have taken
hours upon hours like the blind
poet for thinking that loop

of thought you've become so
accustomed to? What is it like?

It is like coming to a resting place
& not stopping for a single sip
of water or morsel of food,

or even a single glance, say, at
the view, hurtling the body
hiking up the next ridge

where it will also fail
to pause. It is like the mind
finding a machine-like

rhythm & repetition & still
not making any progress
save for its own productions,

some of which you are sure
are not worth squandered
sleep, eyes shut to the day's

detritus. It is like getting
into the habit of being awake
even with the lights low,

of finding that brightness
inside you can't imagine
ever wanting to turn off.

ASK ME

after William Stafford

Some time when Santa
Ana winds blow out in
seventy mile-an-hour
gusts, ask me what I've
destroyed, how many
breezes touched my
face, trusts I betrayed,
how they threw me one
way or the other.

I will hear what you say
over even the strongest
breath & groan of trees,
their branches rubbing
out sound like the creaks
of our house. We know
already what can happen,
how much can get lost,
how the wind says, *but
at what cost?*

THREE TOASTS FOR MY MOTHER

for George Yatchisin

Dehydration coupled with the fact
she hates water means I must find
ways to get her to sip at the surface

of her life: *another toast to all*
the bones I didn't break—
which causes her to shake

her head, &, also ask, *what*
about all the ones you did?
which is fair enough though

all I'm getting are drops on lips,
a mere wetting of the tongue, &
what she needs are gulps to keep

her body flush with what it must
have to stay alive. Somehow
she got all the way to 85 drinking

six cups of coffee a day &
nothing else. No use my
thinking how strange it is

she hates the taste of water
& all those beverages others
consume daily. A toast, then,

to the river in her body she
doesn't like to drink from,
even now when it's a matter

of life & death. She'd
rather take a last breath
then take another sip

from this plastic cup
I've offered her again.
To Life, I say, & she's

still hooked to that idea
in spite of herself, so we
briefly celebrate together

that tie that binds, that
still seductive tether she'd
just as soon, & will, forget.

LEARNING TO LOVE WHAT'S ALREADY LOST

after Shirley Geok-Lin Lim; for my mother

Because solace in the desert is rimless sky,
navigating by constellations instead of a
single star you've been taught will resemble

truth. Because an army surplus tent sleeps
ten but your family transported out of the city
doesn't crowd out consciousness with number

but scarcity. Because dehydration's better
than drowning, thirst preferable to sudden
saturation, because lizards conserving energy

in the heat remind you that meditation's of a
mind to slow down, to find out even a few drops
can sustain you until the next day. Because

the taxidermist in Needles said that he could
stuff the life back into people's pets like
nobody's business, & because it was his business

to do so. Because sometimes in desolate places
creatures are the only companions we have,
dead or alive, wanted unreasonably, like the

stuffed bear one brings to a party populated
by grizzlies. By now you're thinking you've lost
more childhood illusions than you can count &

that it can amount to more than stuffed
animals, to bodies stuffed beyond their
capacity to contain life. Because, still,

they look so life-*like*, even in your wild
imagination, the ones you've still lost,
the ones you take to bed with you

at night. Because you leave on a light
for your sons coming in late, not because
they need it but because you do. Because

it's true you'll lose them anyway or, more
likely, they'll lose you. Because they'll
sip at the rim of your stories when you're

gone & sustain themselves on them until
flooded with memories that now also
belong to them. Because a mind lost

to itself is also most present, absence
a way of no longer belonging to the
known world. Because no other creature

panics in
such a
situation.

LATE NOTE TO WONDER WOMAN

In memory-care you might
forget five minutes ago
but remember that time
your mother, fiercely
teaching you a lesson,
held your hand in flame

for a three count to stop
you from touching
the stove.
Ten minutes ago *I*
was holding your hand
which to you was still

raw, blistered, & I felt
so much tenderness in
that moment it did not
even matter you could
not remember my name.
I was taking care of you,

Wonder Woman,
& for once there

was nothing
for you to
do any
more.

DISSENT

In the memory-care unit
I remind my mother that
I hate Brussels sprouts &

she says what she always
did say to me at dinner:
nonsense! Everyone

loves Brussels sprouts.
I never did find out what
Brussels had to do with it.

I held my seat & tongue all
through dinner, refusing to
eat them, until, at midnight

my mother sent me to bed.
Do you remember what you
said next morning, I ask her,

that if I didn't eat them for
breakfast I would get them
rectally? Of course she re-

members. Ever the rebel
I tell her for the first time
I wrapped those warmed-

up sprouts in my napkin,
flushed them down-toilet
before school, letting her

think that she had won.
We both laugh. *You're
still a bad kid*, she says.

A GOOD MAN

mothering his father, lifting
him out of the rolling chair
in which he's been sitting

into this other one he spends
most of his last days in,
documenting, as ex-doctors do,

his own demise. Today
it's a thread of memory
he found in a movie:

Jimmy Fallon waiting
for Drew Barrymore
to find her way back

to her seat in Fenway,
& Harvey's not sure
whether he's in the film

or out of it. I watch as you
bring him back home to
himself, to his frail body,

his still-sharp mind, make
him laugh so hard he can't
speak or chew the bagel

you've brought him. As
if dying's this slow dance
you're doing with him,

holding him closer than
he's ever wanted, leading
him through these final

steps, lifting him, so
tenderly, into the next
place, some ball-park

he's been dreaming about
where, again, he's the star
of the show. I watch you

help him grow into the man
he wants to become, maybe
just this one who, simply,

loves his son, wants him near
& dear during his last days,
settled & seated where *she*

can still find him.

YOUNG GIRL IN PURSUIT

After a painting by Marc Chagall

My father was a young boy in pursuit
of fast surpassing his own father's
death, his family born in the same

village, Vitebsk, as Chagall, where,
he said, after all, there was only one
synagogue so their families surely

would have met. My sister did once
send one of her own acrylics to this
painter from TV, who, for only

$9.99 said she had genuine talent
& also that she should buy his
book to become even better.

It was a painting of a unicorn.

There are a few
floating horses in Chagall's
work but none with horns

that I remember. In this
one there is an old woman
floating in the wild mane

of the girl's hair, as if to
remind her that pursuit
of wildness in youth is an

illusion. She might even be
a peasant, while the girl
whose hair she inhabits is

surely a performer— circus,

says the curator, though I'm

thinking, burlesque, "heavy
make up," & fanciful dress
being the best a museum

curator can do, a public
being what it is. In any
case she's running with

her golden hair toward
edges of a golden frame,
escaping the same village

as my father's father who
is going to die young, who
is hoping, like her perhaps,

that color alone

will carry them

along to a next

wilder home.

RAIL YARD

after a monotype print by Tony Askew

Sometimes you catch a glimpse
from your seat: graffiti on rail
cars, freight being unloaded,
locomotives moving toward

the next coupling, steel track
stretching out in the four
directions & then some. If
you've slept in one chances are

your clothes were on your back,
you were looking for freight-cars
empty enough for laying down
a new life, & maybe free enough

of rage against newcomers room
might still be made for some
other vagabond looking for
another way on & out of here.

:: :: :: ::

One night
in Gare du
Nord—one
part rail-
station one
part yard—
I spread
my bag out
against the
winter cold
on a wood
floor, & one
with more
claim to it
made sure
I knew it by
hammering
down blade
of his knife
by my head
in a way
that did
not say,
blood so
much as
not even
a finger
beyond

here. I
was in
fear for
my life
though
for once
at least
not in a
place I
knew.

: : : : : : : :

It's true: I've always longed to pull
the switch, ditch new railcars for
old, spray-painted ones where

signatures & stencils & tags
emerge out of dark as if into
light, the bright selves we

all long to die into among
ones who are maybe even
tracking that final transit.

NOT AS SEEN ON TV

(protest, Lower Ninth Ward)

The neighborhood before hurricane,
for example, houses built by owner's
hands & handed down through
generations, pride of place, that way
late sunlight moved through heavy
air so slowly it seemed to bless
the night to come. 14,000 souls
in just one small part of a whole
city of New Orleans.

Many hundreds, maybe even
thousands of homeowners
without titles to the homes
inherited hand-to-hand
from one life to the next
without formalities, no
need for contracts, for
titles or deeds, all those

people with nothing
to show for it save
a trailer with no
utilities.

When not close
to half of what
you once loved
comes back to
you it feels like
empty lots filled
with trash left
there since the
water receded,

you protest,
sign bitterness,
march for lives
you left behind
not as seen on
TV, where
Habitat for
Humanity
is shown re
vitalizing a
city's lower
ninth ward
no longer
existing in
the way it
once did,
by hand,

handing
it down
before
white
army's
levees
broke.

PRAYER

Let even winter light linger on floor
long enough for the dog to find it,
let some of the snow drift in beneath
a closed door with cold air because
it is good to remember that some
are sleeping in lairs tonight. Let
the old fight lay down its weapons,
surrender to something else we
always knew was there— an embrace,
her hair brushing your face, the soft
air of his voice finding its way into
your inner ear. Even after all these
years, may the world find you out
again & again, like lost souls seeking
salvation in this world they left behind
& sometimes even finding a halo of
warm light to sleep in.

A WISH IN THE MIDDLE AGES

In Memory of Elaine Lieberman

May I always see light slanting
through windows just as
you did, as if welcoming

everything from the outside
in should be part of each day.
May I live each minute as if

it matters: sewing new seat-
cushions, hanging a string
of reflecting stones as if

suspended in air. May I
suspend sadness long as
it takes & also embrace its

weight long as *that* lasts,
holding near to bone all
rituals & artifacts that

make up a life. & when
time comes to give them
all away, may I open my

clenched hand & do so,
palm up, offering every
thing I have, every

thing I have
ever been.

ACKNOWLEDGEMENTS

Grateful acknowledgment to publications where some of these poems first appeared, in some cases in slightly different versions:

"Learning to Love What's Already Lost" & "The Body" appeared in Wayfarer; "What I Want" & "Blessing the Migrations" appeared in *Deep Times*; "Three Toasts for My Mother," Dissent," Freedom," "Ode to My Grandfather's Hands," & "Ode to My Daughter's Feet" appeared in *Fledgling Rag*; "Rail-Yard" appeared in *Demon Press'* anthology, *Leaving*; "While Walking in the Butterfly Pavilion" appeared in Thought Crime Publications' anthology, *Not My President*; and "To My Doppelganger" appeared in *The Current.* "No Deposit Zone" was commissioned by and first heard on NPR as part of their "One Square Mile" series.

A heartfelt thank you to Martín Prechtel for his permission to use his words, "grief bed" in the title of this book. His teachings on grief & praise, among many other things, together with his particular and generous way of moving through the world remain deeply compelling & inspiring.

As always, thanks with a bow to Shin Yu Pai for her alertness to my poetic practice & willingness to offer feedback. This book is better for her keen ear & intelligence. Thanks also to Sara Nolan for her willingness to read & comment.

Thank you to Leslie Browning & all of the other good people at Homebound Publications for shepherding this book from manuscript to press.

Finally, deep gratitude to Sarah Benjamin, a poet in her own right, for offering insightful feedback at just the right moment. Thank you, dearest daughter, for your love & clarity.

ABOUT THE AUTHOR

Rick Benjamin lives on Chumash land in Goleta, California, and tries to remind himself of that fact that each day as he walks ancient trails near his house. Currently teaching a range of courses at the University of California Santa Barbara, ranging from poetry and community, the wild literature of ecology, and the literatures of both social and juvenile justice, he also finds himself working among elders, with middle-school students at a local Boys and Girls Club, in art museums and in youth detention facilities. Among his works are the books of poetry, *Passing Love, Floating World,* and *Endless Distances.* He has just recently finished both another manuscript of poems, *A Few of a Number of Accurate Answers,* as well as a book about how poetry works and helps us to do the work of our lives. Rick lives with his partner of many years, Margaret Klawunn, and mostly in reach of their twin sons, Gil and Luke, and daughter, Sarah. He served as the Poet Laureate of Rhode Island from 2012 – 2016.

HOMEBOUND
PUBLICATIONS

We are an award-winning independent publisher founded in 2011 striving to ensure that the mainstream is not the only stream. More than a company, we are a community of writers and readers exploring the larger questions we face as a global village. It is our intention to preserve contemplative storytelling. We publish full-length introspective works of creative non-fiction, literary fiction, and poetry. *Fly with us into our 10th year.*

WWW.HOMEBOUNDPUBLICATIONS.COM

Printed in the USA
CPSIA information can be obtained
at www.ICGtesting.com
JSHW080002150824
68134JS00021B/2224